EARTH MATERIALS AND SYSTEMS

EROSION

by Tamra B. Orr

PEBBLE
a capstone imprint

Pebble Explore is published by Pebble, an imprint of Capstone.
1710 Roe Crest Drive
North Mankato, Minnesota 56003
www.capstonepub.com

Library of Congress Cataloging-in-Publication Data
Names: Orr, Tamra, author.
Title: Erosion / Tamra B. Orr.
Description: North Mankato, MN : Capstone Press, [2021] | Series: Earth materials and systems | Includes index. | Audience: Grades 4-6
Identifiers: LCCN 2020000829 (print) | LCCN 2020000830 (ebook) | ISBN 9781977123787 (hardcover) | ISBN 9781977126788 (paperback) | ISBN 9781977124159 (pdf)
Subjects: LCSH: Erosion—Juvenile literature.
Classification: LCC QE571 .O77 2021 (print) | LCC QE571 (ebook) | DDC 551.3/02—dc23
LC record available at https://lccn.loc.gov/2020000829
LC ebook record available at https://lccn.loc.gov/2020000830

Image Credits
iStockphoto: halbergman, 23, MaxKolmeto, 12, nantonov, 11; Shutterstock Images: Alexxxey, 9, Anek Krachangphat, 15, Anton_Ivanov, cover, Elena Arrigo, 7, Hang Dinh, 18, IrinaK, 28, Kriachko Oleksii, 24, mariyaermolaeva, 5, Salvador Maniquiz, 27, Stephen Barnes, 16, T.Fritz, 19, trekandshoot, 20, Trphotos, 8, Valentin Valkov, 17
Design Elements: Shutterstock Images

Editorial Credits
Editor: Charly Haley; Designer: Jake Nordby; Production Specialist: Joshua Olson

All internet sites appearing in back matter were available and accurate when this book was sent to press.

Printed in the United States of America.
PA117

TABLE OF CONTENTS

Words in **bold** are in the glossary.

What Is Erosion?

Erosion is the process of nature changing Earth. Wind blows dirt away. Heat makes rocks crack and break. Rivers wear down the land they flow through. The water carries rocks and dirt to new places.

Erosion is always happening. But it usually happens too slowly for us to see. It forms valleys. It shapes coastlines and mountains. It wears away everything from the tallest mountain to the longest beach. It changes the land over millions of years.

Ocean waves shape coastlines through erosion.

Where Is Erosion?

Erosion happens all over the world. Water changes land near oceans and lakes. Rivers change the land too. **Glaciers** are giant pieces of ice. They change the land in the coldest places on Earth. Rain and wind change land everywhere.

Oceans, lakes, and rivers are found all over the world. Water shapes the land along oceans and lakes. Rivers cut through land. They also move dirt and rocks.

Rivers can cut deep valleys into land.

Glaciers are in the world's coldest places. Glaciers move very slowly. They change the land when they move.

Wind changes land that is not protected by plants and trees. This happens most in deserts. A lot of desert land is flat. There are no trees or hills. Wind blows fast across flat land. This makes huge sandstorms in deserts. The sand hits rocks. It changes the shape of the rocks.

How Does Erosion Happen?

Many things in nature cause erosion. Water is one of these. It changes land in many ways. Ocean waves move sand on a beach. This changes the beach over time.

Rainfall hits rocks. It slowly wears them away. **Acid** in rain can make holes in rocks. Rain and snow wash away dirt too. They move the dirt into rivers.

Rivers flow through land. The moving water breaks up the rock and dirt it touches. The rock becomes small pieces. The water carries rocks from one place to another.

Sometimes water gets into cracks in rocks. This can happen because of snow or rain. The water in the cracks can freeze. It gets bigger when it becomes ice. This makes the cracks bigger. The rocks can break apart.

Ocean water can also sink into cracks in rocks on the shore. Eventually the water dries up. It leaves behind salt. The salt can build up in the cracks. It breaks apart the rock over time. The pieces may be washed away by water. They may be blown away by wind.

Wind is another part of nature that changes land. Wind blows every day. It moves dirt and rocks from one place to another. This changes the land over time. Wind is what makes tall sand **dunes** in deserts.

sand dune

Wind erosion affects farms. Wind carries away the **topsoil**. Topsoil is dirt that is good for plants to grow. **Crops** won't grow well without topsoil. Farmers try to keep their land safe from erosion.

When glaciers move, they flatten land. They make valleys. They shape mountains. They gather dirt and rocks as they move. This makes the glaciers heavier and faster. They can change the land more.

Hot weather changes the land too. Rocks get hot when the sun shines on them. The heat can make the rocks crack. The rocks become weaker. The rocks break into smaller pieces over time. Wind and water carry the pieces away.

A force called **gravity** also changes the land. People cannot see it. But it pulls everything toward the center of Earth. It is why something falls to the ground when you drop it.

Gravity helps erosion because it pulls rocks and dirt to the ground. This is what happens in a **landslide**. Chunks of rock or dirt fall off the side of a mountain or cliff.

Why Is Erosion Important?

Living things help erosion. Plants and animals change the land. People do too. But erosion also helps living things. It shapes the land around us.

Some beautiful landforms were made by erosion. The Grand **Canyon** in Arizona is one of these. The Colorado River dug into the land for millions of years. This made the deep canyon. The canyon is many miles long. Plants and animals live there. They would not have a home without erosion.

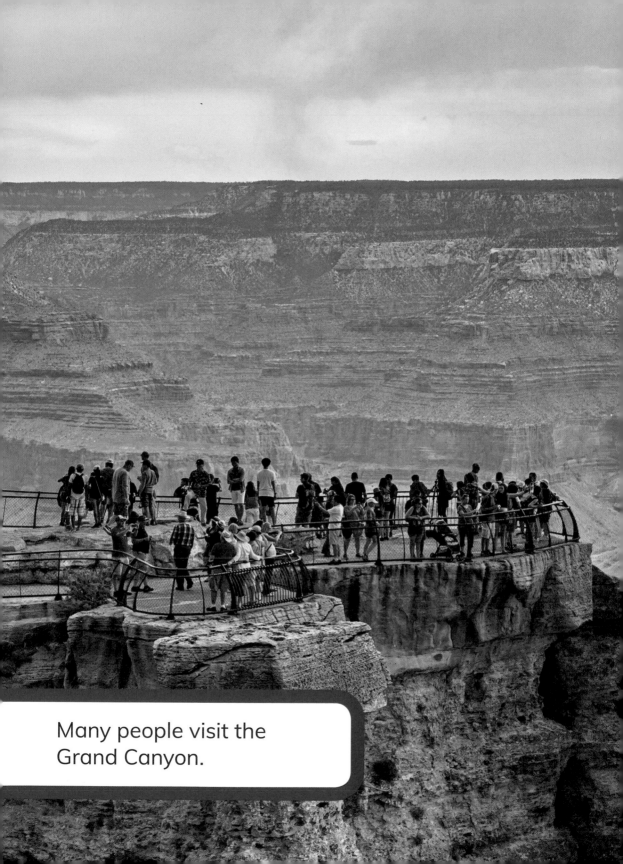

Many people visit the Grand Canyon.

There are many ways that living things change the land. Have you ever seen a dandelion growing out of a crack in a rock? This is an example of how plants cause erosion. Sometimes plants grow in cracks in rocks. The cracks get bigger as the plants grow. The rock breaks apart over time. Then wind or rain carries the pieces away.

Animals like moles and gophers also change the land. They dig into the ground. This breaks up the dirt. It becomes easier for rain or wind to carry the dirt away.

Even people make erosion happen. People cut down forests. They move dirt to build things on the land. Doing these things makes it easier for wind and rain to move the dirt. This changes the land.

Erosion can be harmful or helpful. It is harmful when it damages the land we need for growing crops. But it is helpful when it makes homes for plants and animals.

Erosion is how nature changes the land. It can even create beautiful landforms over millions of years. Erosion is always happening all around us.

Glossary

acid (A-suhd)—a substance that sometimes is found in water; acid can wear away rock

canyon (KAN-yuhn)—a very deep river valley

crop (KROP)—a food plant grown in large amounts

dune (DOON)—a sand hill made by wind

glacier (GLAY-shur)—a huge sheet of ice found in mountain valleys or polar regions

gravity (GRAV-uh-tee)—a force that pulls all things toward the center of Earth

landslide (LAND-slide)—when dirt and rocks fall suddenly from the side of a mountain or hill

topsoil (TOP-soyl)—the top or surface layer of soil; topsoil is good for planting because it contains decaying leaves, grass, and other organic matter

Read More

Higgins, Nadia. *Wind and Water Shape the Land.* North Mankato, MN: Cantata Learning, 2018.

Machajewski, Sarah. *Storms, Floods, and Erosion.* New York: PowerKids Press, 2018.

McAneney, Caitie. *Weathering and Erosion.* New York: Britannica Educational Publishing, 2018.

Internet Sites

DK Find Out!: Rivers
https://www.dkfindout.com/us/earth/rivers

Kids Discover: Erosion! The Ever-Changing Earth
https://www.kidsdiscover.com/teacherresources/erosion-ever-changing-earth

PBS Learning Media: Water Erosion
https://tpt.pbslearningmedia.org/resource/nat08.earth.geol.eros.erosion/nature-water-erosion

Index